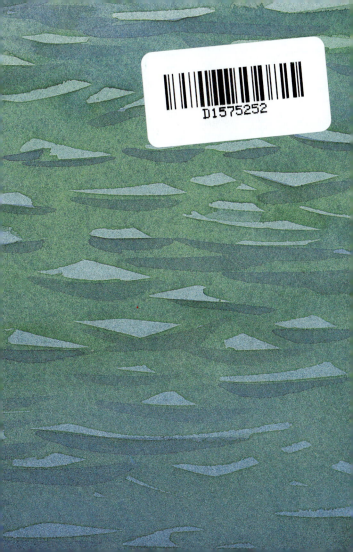

D1575252

Dolphins

MAGIC *of the* OCEAN

Warner Treasures is a trademark of
Warner Books, Inc.

Warner Books, Inc.,
1271 Avenue of the Americas,
New York, NY 10020

 A Time Warner Company

Printed in Mexico
First Printing: March 1995
10 9 8 7 6 5 4 3 2 1

ISBN: 0-446-91008-2

Dolphins

by Barbara Jane Zitwer

MAGIC of the OCEAN

Illustrations by Robbin Gourley

WARNER ⓦ TREASURES ™

PUBLISHED BY WARNER BOOKS

A TIME WARNER COMPANY

DELPHINIDAE

*D*ELPHINIDAE IS THE LATIN WORD for dolphins, who are part of the huge family that includes whales and porpoises. There are over fifty species of dolphins. They are smaller than whales, and all have tiny teeth which they grab their prey with. They are friendly, and we know the most about them because we have been able to study them more than their cousin, the whale. Because of their small size and friendly nature, many dolphins are in captivity in aquatic parks and in scientific reserves where they can be studied.

They all have small flippers, a dorsal fin, and tails that move up and down. They have a highly developed sense of sound and a sonar system that helps them navigate in the ocean.

They give birth to one calf at a time every few years and nurse their young. They're protective of their young, who stay alongside their mothers for up to three years.

Dolphins, like whales and porpoises, definitely have a great sense of loyalty to each other. They stand by injured mem-
bers

of their group, protecting them from their ene-
mies. They support each other and even keep each
other afloat if a member of the group is hurt.
Dolphins act in an excited manner in order to pro-
tect each other. They swim violently and create
whirlpools of water surrounding a threatened animal. They seem to do anything possible to help
each other in times of danger but they also share
happiness and food. Dolphin mothers are particularly loyal to their babies.

Dolphins are found in waters all over the world.
Some varieties are found only in certain areas of the
world but the bottlenose, the most common dolphin, lives everywhere except the arctic.

WE ARE SO DIFFERENT; YET WE ARE THE SAME

THERE ARE NUMEROUS VARIETIES
of dolphins and they range from light gray
to pure white to striped. Some are very small,

others very large. Some are blind; some have better eyesight than deers, who are renowned for their keen vision. Some dolphins have long skinny beaks and sharp teeth; others have no beaks and rounded foreheads. Some have humps on their backs, some are sleek, and others are in between. Dolphins live in rivers, lakes, oceans. They're found everywhere there is water all over the world. Some can jump higher than twenty feet into the air and can dive to a depth of over a thousand feet; others go round and round in shallow rivers.

Some dolphins are spotted like dalmatians. Some are striped like tigers. Some do better axis spins in the air than any Olympic skater! There are even dolphins that are fish, not mammals, and you might have eaten them because they are delicious.

BOTTLENOSE DOLPHINS

THESE ARE THE MOST FAMILIAR TO us because they have been portrayed in so many children's books, films, and TV shows. The most famous dolphin of the 1960s TV show *Flipper* was a bottlenose. The six dolphins who portrayed Flipper on the small screen were so similarly cute, with a light silver color, ever-present smiles and cheerful personalities, that viewers couldn't distinguish that "Flipper" was actually Flippers.

Bottlenoses are among the only dolphins that consistently mate with other dolphin species. Either they don't discriminate, or they have an unusually strong sex drive. Many baby dolphins born in aquariums or oceanariums are the product of a bottlenose father and another species of mother. Put four male bottlenoses in a tank with a female killerwhale, and chances are the whale will get pregnant.

Dolphins

Calves are born singing, and nurse for up to thirty months. They are very attached to their mothers. Each dolphin has its own signature song and very original whistle or sound. Gestation of a bottlenose is about twelve months, and a newborn calf is three and a half feet long. Another female helps the mother with the birth, and the calf usually makes its way to the air on its own. A calf is only helped if it is in trouble.

Bottlenoses are rare among dolphins in that they have excellent vision both in and out of the water. Their eyesight is compared to the excellent sight of deers and antelopes. Perhaps it is so good because they feed on flying fish and need to see well in the air in order to eat. They use their great eyesight in captivity to catch and throw objects, leap out of the water to take a fish from a trainer's hand, or even watch television!

Once, some dolphin trainers noticed that the dolphin in his tank was swimming in a frenzy while watching TV, taking a ball and throwing it high in the air. They couldn't understand this peculiar behavior until they saw what the animal was watching—it was a baseball game!

Bottlenose dolphins take little cat naps day and night.

INTELLIGENCE

WHAT MAKES AN ANIMAL intelligent? The size of its brain? What it does and how it communicates? How it applies what it learns? Under these definitions one might think that dolphins are the smartest animals in the kingdom. Their brains are larger than humans' brains. They have adapted perfectly to their environment, and they adjust, communicate, socialize, and have compassion for each other. We are learning every day with more research how truly intelligent dolphins are, and many scientists believe them to be smarter than apes, perhaps smarter than humans.

Their ability to mimic sounds is an ability that dolphins share only with humans. They can be taught to communicate with humans and learn a few sentences of our language. We know that dolphins communicate with each other, and oceanographers and experts in dolphin study

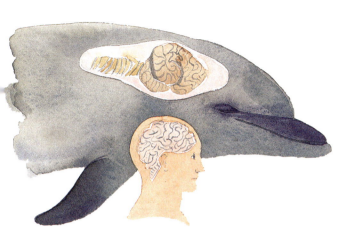

are currently working on communicating with our cousins of the sea.

OPPIAN WROTE IN A.D. 200 THIS powerful plea:

The hunting of dolphins is immoral, and that man can no more draw nigh to the gods as a welcome sacrifice nor touch their altars with clean hands, but pollutes those who share the same roof with him, who willingly devises destruction for the dolphin. For equally with human slaughter the gods abhor the deathly doom of the monarchs of the deep.

SINGING DOLPHINS

IT IS A MYSTERY HOW DOLPHINS make sounds, since they have no vocal cords! Still they make the greatest variety of sounds such as clicking, yelping, barking, squeals, yaps, and many others. They can even make two different kinds of sounds at the same time. Their sound-making is extremely complex. Dolphins have adapted to their environment, the ocean, which is limited in light, and where the ability to make sounds and use internal sonar is key to their survival.

So, how do dolphins make their sounds? One thought is that the sounds emerge through their blowholes. It is the way in which the air passes through their blowholes, or "noses," that creates the variety of sounds. Dolphins have a sac of oil in their foreheads called a melon, which is also a sound transmitter. But how dolphins can make sounds through their foreheads remains a mystery!

Dolphins

Just as dolphins have a phenomenal ability to make various sounds, their sense of hearing is one of the most highly developed and best of any mammal. We know very little about how they hear, because their ears are merely tiny holes at the sides of their heads. Studies show that they hear through their bones.

THEY FLY THROUGH THE AIR WITH the greatest of ease. . . and can also. . .

1. open gates of their watery cages

2. remove hypodermic needles from the body of a fellow dolphin who was being treated with penicillin

3. swim through hoops and follow instructions

4. click, sing, roll over, swim upside down, and do all sorts of swimming on command

5. leap, jump, be aerial artists, and do somersaults in mid-air!

6. play ball, even while blindfolded

7. train their trainer to feed them

8. act in movies

Dolphins

9. play and make up their own fun games

10. throw objects to humans and expect the humans to throw them back, engaging them in a game of catch. Playing and humor are essential parts of dolphin life.

11. play leap-frog over one another
12. play with their sounds to trick each other
13. play basketball

BODY SURFING

MANY DOLPHINS LOVE TO RIDE waves. Just as a city kid on rollerblades hanging on to a bus loves to be taken away on a fast ride, dolphins love to hitch a wave off the bow of a boat. Riding the bow waves lets the dolphins achieve a high speed without using much energy.

Why do they do it when they can swim and leap up to twenty feet in the air on their own? We are constantly learning about dolphins, but it is understood that they are playful creatures. They like to socialize and interact with boats and people, and it could be that they just like the fun of it. It's been reported that dolphins have ridden a boat's waves for hours at a time before tiring.

THE MYTH OF THE DOLPHIN

DIVINER THAN THE DOLPHIN IS nothing yet created; for indeed they were aforetime men and lived along with mortals, but by the devising of Dionysos they exchanged the land for the sea and put on the form of fishes.

— Oppian: Halieutica

The story of how dolphins were created is found in the earliest Greek legends. Here are two Greek myths that introduced dolphins to the world.

Dolphins

Dionysus, the god of wine, hired a boat to travel from the island of Ikaria to that of Naxos. After he was on board, he realized that the sailors were really a bunch of vicious pirates and that they had planned to kidnap him and sell him as a slave. When he uncovered their plot, he became enraged, turned the oars of the ship into snakes, filled the boat with leaves and vines, and drove the sailors to insanity. They all fell overboard and turned into dolphins, so they could never do him or humans any harm again.

After some time, these dolphins became kind and helpful, and it was Poseidon, the king of the sea, who discovered their usefulness. While searching for his bride, Amphitrite, Poseidon was helped by dolphins to find her. The dolphins brought Poseidon to the cave she was hiding in, and because of that the king bestowed the highest and greatest honor on dolphins — he named a constellation after them. In the Northern Hemisphere, the constellation Dolphin can be

✒ℳ21

seen in July in the southeastern sky, between Aquila and Pegasus. The way the Greeks wrote the word *dolphin* is a beautiful rendering of how they felt about these creatures:

$$\delta\epsilon\lambda\phi\grave{\iota}\varsigma$$

DOLPHINS

"ON PLANET EARTH, MAN HAS always assumed that he was more intelligent than dolphins because he had achieved so much — the wheel, New York, wars and so on — whilst all the dolphins had ever done was muck about in the water having a good time. But conversely, the dolphins had always believed that they were far more intelligent than man—for precisely the same reasons." From Douglas Adams' *The Hitchhiker's Guide to the Galaxy*.

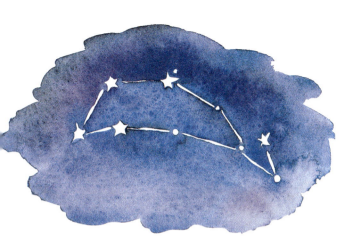

SUSU DOLPHINS

THE REMARKABLE SUSU DOLPHINS are totally blind. They live in rivers and are only found in India. Compensating for their lack of sight, they have intense and highly developed sonar systems and make sounds that reverberate toward any objects in the water and then bounce back to their inner ears. Their sonar and sounds allow them to swim freely and exist quite well.

Dolphins

It is conjectured that susus lost their sight millions of years ago when they found themselves cut off from the ocean and living in the riverbeds of India. Their environment was so dirty and silt-filled that as centuries passed, their eyesight became useless.

Susus are very small compared to some other dolphins, measuring about six or seven feet in length at the most. They have tiny teeth and long

beaks. During mating season, rice farmers along the Ganges and smaller rivers can observe intense flurries of water movement and whirlpools created by dolphins mating. A female susu gives birth to one calf at a time, and the newborn calf is about a yard long. Susus are small grayish-blue animals that lick and cluck their way through life— they can only swim in circles, and are incapable of swimming in a straight line.

DOLPHINS AS HEROES AND FRIENDS

DOLPHINS WERE MENTIONED IN Shakespeare's *Twelfth Night*. In the first act of the play, a poet and musician named Arion was helped ashore by a dolphin after pirates threw him overboard. Arion was no god, but a singer who was blessed with the most melodic voice. All envied Arion his talent, and everyone loved him. After a successful tour around Greece, sailing home, he was captured by pirates and thrown overboard, just like Dionysus. His captors allowed Arion a last request, which was to sing his last song. He sang a shrill, beautiful melody, and then he dove into the sea. A dolphin heard him sing and carried him safely ashore. When he returned home and reported his misadventure to the king, the pirates were arrested, and all his riches were restored to him.

From the time of the earliest Greek and Latin myths, dolphins became known and regarded as

great friends to men and, especially, young boys.
Stories were told of how dolphins carried young
boys to and from school. In one story, a dolphin
tried to save a young boy from drowning, and
when he carried the boy's body to shore, he too
flipped himself down beside the body on the sand.

He died alongside the child, thinking it only right that their life and death be shared. This story comes from the island of Iasos, where the people made a coin with the image of the dolphin and boy on it.

The dolphin appears in many works of art and on coins from early Greek and Roman times. A Dionysos Cup by Exekias from 540 B.C. is decorated with dolphins. The image of a dolphin is found on a fifth-century Greek gem and also on a Roman coin dating from 74 B.C.

ARISTOTLE'S OBSERVATIONS

A RISTOTLE WAS NOT ONLY A philosopher but a scientist as well, and he particularly liked marine biology. While in his forties, he lived on the island of Lesbos and studied dolphins. Aristotle lived four centuries before Christ and wrote in his book *History of Animals* many observations that are relevant today. He

knew that dolphins were different
from fish, could breathe through
lungs, and nursed their
young.

DOLPHINS ARE BLESSED

THESE CREATURES BRING A
blessing with them. No day in which they
have played a part is like other days. I first saw
them at dusk, many years ago, on the way to
Mount Athos. A whole troop appeared alongside
the steamer, racing her and keeping us company
for three-quarters of an hour. Slowly it grew

darker and as night fell the phosphorescent water turned them into fishes of pale fire. White-hot flames whirled from them. When they leapt from the water they shook off a million fiery diamonds, and when they plunged, it was a fall of comets spinning down fathom after fathom — league upon league of dark sky, it seemed — in whirling incandescent vortices, always to rise again; till at last, streaming down all together as though the heavens were falling and each trailing a ribbon of blazing and feathery wake, they became a faraway constellation on the sea's floor. They suddenly turned and vanished, dying away along the abyss like ghosts.

    Patrick Leigh Fermor, *Mani: Travels in the Southern Peloponnese*

    In early Christian teachings dolphins symbolized swiftness, diligence, and love.

DR. DOLPHIN

THERE IS A GREAT AMOUNT OF research and study being conducted that is revealing how dolphins can help reduce stress in humans, teach autistic and emotionally disturbed children, and help us in numerous other medical and therapeutic areas. Dolphins may provide important alternatives to traditional teaching and medical practices.

Dolphins have the most highly developed sense of inner sonar and telepathic abilities. The way they communicate with each other is extremely sophisticated, and it has been proven in many circumstances that dolphins can communicate with children and adults with problems when no other treatment has worked.

Experts feel that water therapy alone is very beneficial, because it immediately reduces the stress on our bodies. We are gestated in a fluid-filled womb for nine months, so each time we

return to the water, we re-create that original
peaceful and natural experience of complete relax-
ation and safety.

By just swimming along with dolphins,
humans feel a great sense of happiness and well-
being, which can last for up to two weeks. It is also
believed that because of their strong inner sonar
system, dolphins can scan our bodies. Body scan-
ning, described as feeling like an inner massage,
gives one a tingling feeling all over. A
swimmer can feel the animal's
vibrations, which seem to be
beneficial.

A most unusual
case was reported in
an aquatic park,

when a swimmer was hit in the ribs by a genuinely friendly dolphin. The shocked, hurt swimmer was rushed to the hospital. When an X-ray of her ribs was taken, a tumor showed up just below where the dolphin had hit her. This amazing fact opens up incredible possibilities. Can dolphins detect a tumor with their natural scanners, and can their powers eventually be focused into shrinking one?

All over the world, oceanariums, aquatic research centers, and scientists are beginning to seriously study these amazing creatures and their curative powers. Their psychic, telepathic, and sonar abilities are only just being discovered. In the future, we might go to dolphins to be cured of anxiety, depression, cancer, arthritis . . . anything is possible.

THE STUFF OF DREAMS

HILDE DOMAIN "REQUEST TO A DOLPHIN" (translated from the German by Michael Butler)

Every night
embracing my pillow like a
    gentle dolphin
I swim farther away.

Gentle Dolphin
in this sea of heartbeats
bear me,

when light dawns,
to a more friendly shore.
Far from the coast of tomorrow.

Dolphins have been the subject of poets and writers since before Aristotle. John Steinbeck wrote of dolphins in his *Sea of Cortez* as did Henry David Thoreau in *Cape Cod* and Dante in his *Inferno*.

Robert Graves, in *The White Goddess,* describes dolphins as one of the "royal fish of Britain, the other being the whale."

In Silvina Ocampo's poem "Dolphins" she expresses their dreamlike quality: "They sink into sleep as they fall to the depth of the sea . . . like our dreams."

For Russian poet Valery Petrov, dolphins represent loneliness in his poem of that title: "As though it weren't enough, it seems, that every one is separately alone."

Lewis Carroll wrote in *Alice in Wonderland*:

"No wise fish would go anywhere without a porpoise."

D. H. Lawrence wrote "They Say the Sea Is Loveless," but he knew and felt otherwise, as we can see from his beautiful poem:

But from the sea
the dolphins leap round Dionysius' ship
whose masts have purple vines,
and up they come with the purple dark of the
rainbows
and flip! they go! with the nose-dive of sheer
delight

Dolphins

Dolphins are not just the theme of long dead poets and writers. The most cutting-edge fiction writers also are enchanted with these creatures.

Marge Piercy's "Another Country" gives this glorious description:
They ride through pleasure and plenty
secure in a vast courtesy
firm enough to sustain a drowning man

Ogden Nash wrote in "The Porpoise":
I kind of like the playful
porpoise,
A healthy mind in a healthy corpus.
he and his cousins, the playful dolphins,
Why they like swimmin
like I like golphin.

Dolphins are the heroes of numerous children's books, and since early Greek and Roman times, dolphins' popularity in literature has grown.

*T*HE *BIG BLUE*, DIRECTED BY LUC
Besson   rating: 3½ dolphins

The theme of Luc Besson's film is the obsession of the young Jacques with dolphins and the ocean. Jacques grows up on a Greek island and has the incredible ability to dive to the depths of the sea for longer than any other human being. As only dolphins and whales do, Jacques is able to lower his heart rate, thereby allowing the blood to flow merely to his head. He can stay submerged under the water for ten minutes at a time and dive to depths of over four hundred feet, stupefying scientists and doctors.

Since his childhood, dolphins have pervaded his dreams, and at the end of the film, he takes his final dive to see what lies below "the big blue." As

*(all available on video)

Dolphins

he swims farther and farther, going beyond all limits set by scientists for deep-sea test diving, when he is beyond all limits of human possibility, he

meets his destiny, a dolphin who beckons him farther along. The film ends with a magnificent image of Jacques swimming out to sea. The ocean shimmers in the moonlight, and a dolphin leaps from the water as he swims farther out to the horizon. Jacques has given up everything — a woman's love, life on land, his friends, his home — for the ocean and his friends the dolphins.

This film is like a Greek myth and is similar to so many stories told and retold over the centuries depicting the magic, the friendship, the harmony of humans and dolphins.

*T*HE *D*AY OF THE *D*OLPHIN, DIRECTED by Mike Nichols, written by Buck Henry; based on Robert Merle's novel of the same title. rating: 2½ dolphins

This is an unusual film about a marine biologist, played by George C. Scott, who is studying the intelligence and linguistic potential of a dolphin named Alpha, and teaches the animal to speak several words. The film clearly depicts these creatures as having extraordinary intelligence and loyalty. Unbeknownst to Scott, the corporation that funds his studies is run by a renegade political group that want to assassinate the

President of the United States. A story that begins as a benign study of dolphins turns into a taut thriller as Scott and his colleagues discover the evil intentions of this group, who kidnap his dolphin and train him to plant a bomb on the presidential vessel. Scott's dolphin, Alpha, and his new mate, Beta, save the day by attaching the bomb to the bad guys' boat instead of planting it on the President's boat.

This scenario might seem far-fetched, but in truth, the Navy has admitted that dolphins were used both in Vietnam and in the Gulf War to place underwater bombs and also to detect mines in rivers and oceans. Dolphins are used by the military for warmongering purposes because of their high intelligence and their abilities. *The Day of the Dolphin* is a cautionary tale; at the end of the film, Scott burns all his documents and life's work and pleads with his beloved Alpha to return to the ocean and never speak to people or return to find him. The dolphin replies, "Love Pa," and swims off. The film is fiction, but many of the facts presented in it are true.

FLIPPER, THE MOVIE
rating: 2 dolphins

For pure camp and sentimental value, *Flipper* is a must.

In the movie, Flipper, ten-year-old Bud and fifteen-year-old Sandy's pet dolphin, is captured by some dolphin hunters looking for animals to train for their aquatic park. They take Flipper over two hundred miles away from his home, but he escapes. The movie shows the adventures of this remarkable dolphin. During his odyssey he saves a deep-sea diver from drowning, helps a sea turtle ensnared in a fisherman's net, saves a pet dachshund from being eaten alive by a crocodile, and more. Wherever Flipper goes, he helps animals and people around him. He's the Superman of the sea.

Dolphins

Meanwhile, Bud and Sandy have convinced their dad, Porter, to drive the two hundred miles to see if the dolphin who saved the diver is their beloved Flipper. At the end of the film, he comes to the aid of Bud, who is trapped in an underwater cave.

The movie has some great underwater footage of dolphins and other animals, and although the dialogue and manner in which all the human scenes are shot are bad 1960s-TV style, real scientific information about dolphins is incorporated into the story. For kids, this is both a fun adventure and a way to introduce them to the wonder of these creatures.

RULES FOR SWIMMING WITH DOLPHINS

IT IS BEST TO SWIM WITH DOLPHINS who are wild and free in their natural habitat, because they are at their peak rather than being emotionally or mentally inhibited by captivity. There has never been a report of a dolphin hurting a person, and they are gentle and intelligent creatures. However, they are creatures of the wild, and there are some rules that should be followed, for their protection and yours, and also to give you the best and most successful experience of being with them.

1. Never wear any jewelry in the water. It can scrape or scratch their sensitive skin and upset them, and if they are cut, an infection can occur that could be deadly.

2. It is important to let the dolphin know that you are a friend and to build a rapport with the animal. The best way is to keep your arms behind your back and allow the animal to get to know

51

you. If you thrust your arms forward, the dolphin might interpret that as a hostile act and react to it.

3. Never use a flash while photographing dolphins underwater. They have very sensitive eyes, and the flash can blind them.

4. Menstruating women should not swim with male dolphins. Dolphins are very active sexually and can be aroused by a woman during this time. It might be extremely unpleasant to have a

group of sexually excited male
dolphins trying to mate with
you!

5. Dolphins
never like to be
manipulated — so be
gentle in the water. Observe
the animals' behavior and rhythm and
get into their flow and movement. Be

relaxed, and try to become one with the animal.

6. Never swim with a dolphin if you have any infections, sickness, or medical problems — this can affect the extremely vulnerable and sensitive dolphin. Only swim with the animals when you are in perfect health!

7. NEVER — EVER — NEVER !!!! stick your finger in the dolphin's blowhole or put your hand near it. The animal breathes through this just as we breathe through our noses. If a dolphin's breathing is threatened, he will defend himself!